RASPBERRY PI

The Absolute Beginner's Guide to Raspberry Pi. Convert Your Computer Into a Phone, Build an Arcade Machine, and More! (2022 Crash Course for Newbies)

Tristram Soto

Congratulations and thank you for ordering a Raspberry Pi.

The chapters that follow will go through all of the various pieces that we'll need to deal with when it comes to the Raspberry Pi device.

This is the ideal gadget for any developer to utilize, and if you learn how to use it correctly, you will discover that it can help you get your feet wet and make it simpler for you to truly jump in and see some results with your programming talents.

In this handbook, we will look at what we can accomplish with the Raspberry Pi, as well as some of the reasons why it is such a useful software to learn how to work with.

We'll start with a good overview of what the Raspberry Pi is all about, as well as some background on where this board comes from and how we're supposed to utilize it.

To assist us get started, we will also spend some time looking at the different perks that come with this equipment.

Then it's time to dive into the specifics of what we can accomplish with this kind of gadget.

We'll go through some of the steps we can take to get this device set up in our own homes, such as getting the operating system to operate on here, configuring the device, and even connecting this to our home wi-fi and other Bluetooth devices if that's what we want to do.

When we're through with that, it's time to move on to some of the navigation that has to take place for us to get this device to act the way we want it to, such as how to browse through all of the files, folders, and menus.

This is where we will need to spend some time learning how to use the Python coding language.

Other languages work with the Raspberry Pi if you choose to use them, but Python is one of the finest possibilities for a newbie who has never done anything with coding and programming.

This handbook will discuss some of the possibilities for utilizing the Python IDLE, and then we will go over some of the fundamentals that we need to understand when it comes to dealing with Python code and developing some of our own along the road.

The next issue on which we should spend some time is how to utilize the Raspberry Pi for some of our programming requirements.

We'll look at several communication protocols and how to conduct some of the interfacing we desire with the Raspberry Pi and other devices of our choosing.

We can next spend some time looking at how to use the GPIO pins on this device and what each one signifies before moving on to some of the tips and techniques that all new programmers should know to get the most out of this device for their requirements.

When it comes time to conduct some of the programming work that we desire, there are a lot of things that we need to keep in mind and comprehend.

However, the Raspberry Pi device is one of the greatest possibilities that we can work with when we are ready to get started, and we want to be sure that everything works as it should for our coding and application models.

When you're ready to learn more about how to work with the Raspberry Pi device and how to write using Python so that you can truly get this gadget to perform properly, check out this handbook to get started.

There are several books on this topic available; once again, thank you for selecting this one!

Every effort has been taken to ensure that it is as full of relevant information as possible; please enjoy it.

Chapter 1:

What is the Raspberry Pi?

There will be a lot of pretty wonderful things available to us in the realm of technology today.

We may discover a variety of programming languages to use while writing code, as well as a variety of tools and accessories that help us get things done.

With all of this technology evolving and changing all the time, novices may feel as if they are falling behind and should give up rather than try.

They are concerned that the task will be too difficult for them to complete.

The cool part about this is that Raspberry Pi will be there to assist fix the situation.

This will be a little computer board, approximately the size of a credit card, that can connect to your computer display or TV.

It will be smaller in size, but it will have a lot of power and can enable individuals of all ages and experience levels with methods to discover how the world of computers works, as well as making it simpler to learn how to work with a range of programming languages, such as Python, C++, and Scratch.

This approach is going to be a lot simpler to work with than some of the other ways of learning to program out there.

It will be simpler than most other programming tools available, and it will offer us a safe environment in which to learn and practice our abilities, even if we are beginners.

To begin, the Raspberry Pi gadget will accomplish whatever that a regular desktop computer would do, such as processing various voices, searching the internet, generating tables, gaming, watching HD films, and so on.

Furthermore, we shall discover that this gadget has the power to interface with the outside world.

There are several digital projects that may be created with this gadget.

This may include houses with cameras on the birds, meteorological stations, and even detectors that parents can use.

As you can see, there is a lot that we need to know when it comes to working with Raspberry Pi, and you will be able to use it for a variety of different projects.

We'll look at some of the available choices for this device and learn some of the code required to get it up and running.

It's incredible what we're capable of when it comes to working with the Raspberry Pi.

It is such a simple item to use, but it really makes a difference in how well we can learn about and deal with computers, as well as how effectively we can go through the process of learning new code and programming languages.

The Specifications You Should Be Aware Of

The next thing we need to look at is some of the specs that we need to know while dealing with the Raspberry Pi.

This will be a little different than what we are accustomed to seeing with some of the other devices that we may wish to work with, but you will discover that it works as you expect.

This section will go through some of the specs you'll need to know for this:

Even though the Raspberry Pi 3 is a smaller device, it has a plethora of components that you will like using with this little computer.

The Raspberry Pi 3 is the third iteration of the Raspberry Pi, and the primary changes between this version and previous versions are as follows:

1. 1.2 GHz quad-core 64-bit ARMv8 CPU

2. Wireless LAN 802.11n

Bluetooth 4.1 is the latest version of Bluetooth, while Bluetooth Low Energy is the latest version of Bluetooth.

In addition to some of the differences between Raspberry Pi 3 and previous generations, there are a few more features that you will like while using this product.

These are some examples:

1. 3D graphics core VideoCore IV

2. Micro SD card reader

3. graphical user interface

4. Interface with the camera

5. A 3.5-mm audio connector and a composite video jack are combined.

Ethernet port No. 6

7. HDMI port with full functionality

40 GPIO pins are available.

9 USB 2.0 ports

1 GB of RAM

Are There Different Raspberry Pi Models?

The next thing we need to look at is if there are many distinct versions

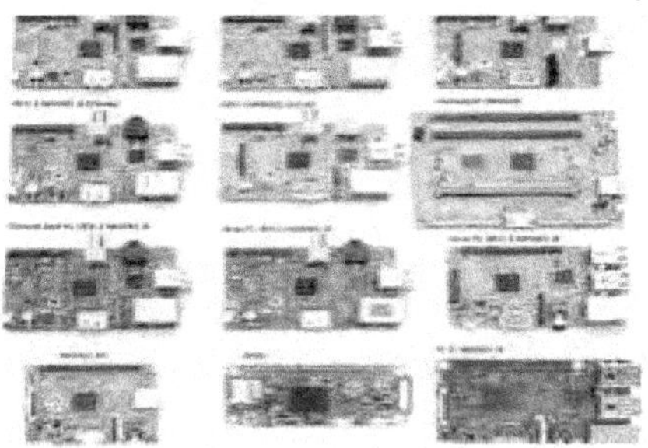

of the Raspberry Pi software that we may use.

The wonderful part is that there are many versions, and the one you choose to work with will depend on the tasks you want to complete and your overall aims.

Right now, the Raspberry Pi 3 is considered the most recent version of this programming option, and it will be capable of handling some of the more complicated types of programming that you would want to undertake.

There are also some additional selections and models that provide some fresh features on which you may depend. A programmer may deal with many different versions and kinds of Raspberry Pi. These include:

- Raspberry PI 1 Model A: This is the original Model A that was released in 2012.

The Plus version was released a few years later and was an upgrade since it featured a bigger hard drive and a cheaper price point than the prior edition.

Raspberry Pi 2 Variant B: The initial edition of this was released in 2012, followed by the Plus model in 2014.

The Model B Plus version was less expensive, and it enabled users to operate with a microSD card rather than the usual SD slot seen in prior models.

- Raspberry Pi Zero: The Raspberry Pi Zero was released in 2015. Because the Zero was supposed to be smaller than some of the previous variants, it had less output and input for the user.

It is, however, the least price of the Raspberry Pi models.

It is now more inexpensive than ever.

When Zero was first released, there were no video input choices.

However, the second version of this was produced in 2016 that had this functionality.

- Raspberry Pi 2: This is the model with the most features compared to any of the previous versions.

It was introduced in early 2015, and it is regarded as one of the family's higher-end models.

Even though it is more expensive, it is still incredibly reasonable, costing just $35.

- Raspberry Pi 3: This is the most recent model in the Raspberry Pi computer series.

It was introduced in early 2016, and it comes with all of the accessories you'll need to get started with this computer.

USB boot capabilities, Bluetooth, and Wi-Fi are some of the extras that are often offered with this model

Keep in mind that these are only a few of the many possibilities available to you when it comes to the Raspberry Pi program.

Even though you may choose from a few ways to make it function, you will notice that they all have a few qualities in common.

For example, you will immediately see that they all come with the Broadcom feature on a chip, and the central processing system that they depend on will have the ARM protocol.

On all versions of the system, there is also a GPU.

Every board will also have at least one USB slot. However, some of them do come with two, three, or even four slots that we may rely on depending on our demands.

You will also see that there are additional slots on your device for phone jacks, HDMI, and composite video output to assist you if you wish to work with audio on some of these tasks as well.

The good news is that the team that worked here to construct and develop many of the models that come with Raspberry Pi will also be in charge of the Raspbian operating system, which will be a terrific operating system to help us get more out of the system.

This operating system will be comparable to what we may find when dealing with Linux, so if you have used that operating system in the past, you will find the Raspbian operating system to be rather familiar.

Another thing to keep in mind is that while working with the Raspberry Pi, you will also be able to work with a few different operating systems.

This system will support different operating systems such as RISC OS, Ubuntu, and Windows, and Linux frequently runs well on it as well.

As a result, you may look through them all and choose the one that best suits your requirements along the road.

The Operating System for the Raspberry Pi

One of the operating systems must be installed in order for us to be able to get the Raspberry Pi device up and running in the way that we want and for it to be useable.

This might be intimidating to deal with if you are unsure of the procedures to follow; the best strategy is to choose an operating system that will fit whatever duties you want to utilize the Raspberry Pi for in the first place.

One thing that may surprise you when you first start here is that there are numerous coding languages and operating systems that really operate on this device, so you have a lot of options for what you want to accomplish with it.

You must browse through and choose the best choice for you, but some of the greatest possibilities that function well with this kind of gadget include:

1. Raspbian: This is the official operating system that this device supports.

This is an easy operating system to use, and if you don't have a preference for one of the other alternatives or have never dealt with one before, you'll find it to be a good choice.

2. Pidora: This is a Fedora Remix operating system that has been slightly modified to function nicely with the Raspberry Pi.

3. RaspBMC: This is an open-source media center that is free to use.

If you just intend to use the device for that purpose, this is a suitable operating system to go with.

4. OpenELEC: This is a tiny Linux-based operating system that performs well on the device.

It can transform your Raspberry Pi into a Kodi media center.

5. RISC OS: This is a very small operating system that is highly quick. This one was created in such a manner that it works best on devices having ARM architecture.

6. Arch: This will be a versatile and lightweight Linux distribution with which you may work.

7. Python: Python is one of the greatest programming languages for beginners to learn.

We will look at some of the codings that you need to be aware of while using Python so that you may develop your own scripts on this device

A Quick Overview of Raspbian

While we're here, we should look at how we might work with the Raspbian operating system.

There are other possibilities, but none will give us the knowledge and convenience of use to interact with the Raspberry Pi that we will discover with the Raspbian operating system.

This is a solid operating system with which we can operate, and it is free, so we won't have to worry about any additional fees.

It will be based on the Debian operating system, so you will be free to utilize it in whatever way you choose to get your devices to function properly.

You will shortly see that the Raspbian operating system will function exactly this way.

It will also include a slew of packages, up to 35,000 in all, in a format that makes them very simple to install on this system.

The Raspbian operating system will allow us to work on all of our projects and observe advancements, and there will be a lot of development activity, which means that these extensions will grow better and better.

This is going to be an operating system with a decent environment that can run on a desktop, so it will appear pretty much the same as some of the other operating systems that you may already be familiar with.

You may also work with some of the available options to guarantee that the applications that are active perform the job for you here.

Using the desktop environment that comes with Raspbian is usually a great touch for individuals who haven't had much experience working with the console that comes with Linux.

Keep in mind that this is going to be a device with a lot of power, but it won't be able to handle some of the larger processes that we see with desktop computers.

This implies that it will be limited in its ability to do certain tasks, such as 4K movies, video editing, and photography, to mention a few.

Even with some of these limits, you'll be surprised at what the Raspbian operating system is capable of.

Because this operating system is seen as a kind of distribution that comes with Linux, you can be certain that your applications will have a few security features and will have more network capabilities.

We must remember that Linux is always a solid choice for an operating system, and you should be able to complete a plethora of tasks with the little Raspberry Pi gadget.

If you choose, you may even bring in a range of alternative operating systems.

Chapter 2

Setting Up the Raspberry Pi

Now that we've covered the fundamentals of the Raspberry Pi device and know what it's all about, as well as a few of its capabilities, it's time to go a little more into how we might utilize it for our purposes.

First, there will be a number of actions that we will need to be able to do to guarantee that this device behaves in the way that we want it to and completes all of the programs that we want along the way.

It takes some time for us to set up this gadget and ensure that it will operate properly.

The good news is that it will not be as difficult as it may seem to someone who is just starting started.

There are a few steps to take, and we need to look at some of the pieces that come with the Raspberry Pi, as well as some of the accessories that we may want to consider bringing in so that we can utilize this properly.

In this chapter, we will look at some of the different components that we need to know in order to get started, how to properly set up the operating system, how to set up all the other parts, and even how to test out the program to ensure that it will work and that it can do the other projects and work with programming that we want.

So, with that in mind, let's get started

What You Need to Know to Get Started with Raspberry Pi

There will be a lot of items that we will need to acquire before we can get started on this entire procedure.

If we want to see this process successfully, we need to have them on hand before we go too far into it.

To begin, we must first get the precise Raspberry Pi device that we want.

When it comes to the Raspberry Pi device, we may also operate with the following supplies:

- An HDMI-capable monitor or television: You'll need to be able to connect the device to a display.As long as it can support HDMI, a television or computer monitor will suffice.There are also other tiny choices that you may use if you choose.
- A mouse and keyboard: These must be connected to a USB port in order to connect to the Raspberry Pi.

  Any kind will do, but they must be able to connect to the gadget so that you can command it.

  We can work with this without the need for a mouse or a keyboard.

  However, since most people are accustomed to using them on their normal computer, having them accessible for use on the Raspberry Pi will make it simpler to get started and can eliminate some of the difficulties that we encounter while using this device.

- MicroSD card and card reader: The Raspberry Pi's operating system does not include a hard drive.

  Instead, it comes pre-loaded with a MicroSD card.

  If you don't acquire one with at least 8GB of storage, you won't be able to do anything with the gadget.

  If you have a card reader on your PC, you're generally good to go.

  If the screen you're using doesn't have this feature, you may buy a card reader online for under $10.

- Power supply: The Raspberry device will be powered via a micro-USB cable.

  This is comparable to what your phone is powered by.

  There are four USB ports to which electricity may be supplied.

  Simply ensure that the power source you choose can provide a minimum of 2.5A of power to the device.

These are only a handful of the several possibilities available to us, and they are the most basic.

We may go through and choose additional aspects depending on the project that we want to work on.

Once we have all of these pieces available and ready to use, we can begin the setup procedure to get the device to operate.

How to Setup an Operating System

To get the gadget to operate properly, we must first ensure that the operating system is downloaded and ready.

Without the operating system, we will only have a gadget that can power on but has a blank screen and does nothing else.

As a result, we must now choose the operating system with which we want to work and proceed to install it.

To begin working on installing the desired operating system, we must first ensure that we have another conventional computer to work with, either a desktop or a laptop.

We want to work with the Raspbian operating system, but we must first install it on one of our ordinary PCs before transferring it to the Pi device via an SD card.

You, as the coder, will now have a few options here, which we will restrict to two.

To begin, ensure that the Raspbian operating system is manually installed on the machine.

This implies you'll need to bring in some external software to get it done, or you'll need to come in with enough coding knowledge to get it all done by entering this into the command line.

NOOBs is the second choice that you may work with, and it is the most frequent option that new programmers like to work with since it is easy to download and install.

Because this is the more appealing choice for many people due to its simplicity, we will examine the essential actions required to make this one a reality below:

- First, we need to pull out the SD card that we want to utilize with the computer's card reader.
- We'll spend a few minutes on our PC downloading the NOOBs.

When we come to this point, we should have a few alternatives to pick from.

You may investigate these alternatives, but for simplicity, we will choose "offline and network install."

This is the option for downloading the Raspbian operating system.

- In certain cases, we will need to format our SD card as FAT to use it.

  If this is the case with your card, you may easily get this formatting utility from the SD Association.

  Look for the section that says "Format Size Adjustment" on the sdcard.org website.

  Make sure that option is turned on in your settings menu, and your card will be ready to go.

- This will be a procedure that will assist us in obtaining a nice zip file to work with.

  You may then remove the operating system from this location.

  When the extraction is complete, be careful to transfer the whole contents of the folder to the SD card.

  When the copying procedure is complete, remove the SD card from the card reader or PC and insert it into the Raspberry device.

We now have an SD card with the Raspbian operating system on it, and that SD card should be in the Raspberry Pi device with which we want to operate.

This will guarantee that we can conduct some of the work that we want with this device since we require that operating system to make everything function.

How Do We Connect Our Raspberry Pi Device?

Now that we've spent the time downloading and installing our operating system, it's time to go through and make sure that every item we're going to utilize with our Pi device can be linked up and correctly connected to it.

This will be a very straightforward phase to do since you will just need to take on all of the components and then connect them into the USB ports already present on our Raspberry Pi.

However, you may find that using the following sequence will ensure that everything is done correctly.

The approach described below is the best to use since it ensures that if you connect a device to your Pi, the Raspberry Pi will be able to identify that device when it starts up.

The following will be the most effective approach to dealing with this device and all of the devices that you wish to work with:

1. Begin by plugging the monitor into the device.
2. Once the display has been detected, connect the keyboard and mouse.
3. If you wish to use an Ethernet cable to connect to the internet, now is the time to do so.
4. Finally, connect the power source you're utilizing.

Because this gadget does not have a power switch, it will turn on as soon as the power source is hooked into it

Installing Raspbian

At this point, we've had a chance to go through the process of copying the operating system to our SD card and getting it ready to go.

But now we need to make sure that everything boots up, particularly the NOOBs that we discussed previously, so that we can utilize our device.

This takes a few minutes, so you should be prepared for nothing to happen right immediately.

The reason for this is because the NOOBs application will take some time to format the SD card it is on and will do a check to ensure that the other elements are properly configured.

Keep this in mind, and don't get too frustrated with the pace here.

Even though it is natural to be enthusiastic at this point and want to utilize the Raspberry Pi, you must take your time and let the NOOBs application to perform all of the required duties.

If you attempt to speed through all of this, or if you try to skip ahead, you will induce corruption in the process, and your system will not function properly.

After the NOOBs application has had a few minutes to complete the required duties, you should observe a little screen appear on the Pi.

This page will prompt us to install the operating system that we want to utilize on the device.

You may choose any of the operating systems you wish here, but we'll stick with the methods we discussed before to accomplish Raspbian.

Some of the measures we'll need to take to make this happen are as follows:

1. Locate the bottom of your console's screen.
    There should be a section where you may pick the keyboard layout as well as the language depending on your location.
2. Look for the Raspbian operating system and tick the box next to it.
    This instructs the operating system to install the operating system.
3. NOOBs will be tasked with installing this operating system. It may take up to 20 minutes to finish this, so be patient. When the Raspbian operating system is uploaded, you will be transported to the Raspbian desktop, where you may configure anything else.

How to Setup the Raspberry Pi

When we come to this stage, the Raspberry Pi device should be set up and ready to go.

You should be able to see your operating system and a pleasant start menu in place when you glance at the device.

However, there are a few more procedures that we must complete before the Raspberry Pi gadget will function properly, and we may begin with them from the start menu.

So, go to the start menu and choose it. The portion for applications may then be selected by clicking on it.

Then click to bring up the file browser.

This is where we can go through and input whatever instructions you want so that the system understands what it is intended to perform.

This will be a similar approach to what other operating systems will use, and we will look at some of the most popular instructions for this as we go through it.

Before we get to those instructions, we need to look at a few more choices for configuring the Raspberry Pi device.

We'll look at some of them today, including how to install and configure the Bluetooth and Wi-Fi capabilities on this device so we can work on other projects and get it to behave the way we want it to in the long run.

How to Connect the Raspberry Pi to Your Home WiFi

When it comes to this gadget, you'll be pleased to learn that connecting the Raspberry Pi to your home Wi-Fi is a breeze.

In reality, you will be able to use many of the same methods to connect the Raspberry Pi to the internet as you would with a standard computer, whether it is a laptop or a desktop computer.

If you've done this before, connecting the Raspberry Pi device will be simple.

To begin, search for the network icon, which should be available in the main menu of your Pi device.

Make a point of clicking on this one.

This will be a basic symbol that looks like two primary computers next to each other, and it should be located somewhere towards the top and to the right of your screen.

When you discover that icon, click on it and then search for the Wi-Fi network that you want to utilize for this.

Click on the network of choice, input the username and password, and wait for it to connect.

And that is all there is to this procedure.

You must ensure that you are using the correct Wi-Fi and that you know the password and username, but after a few seconds of connecting, the Raspberry Pi device will appear as one of your network devices and will be ready to use.

Using Bluetooth to Connect to Devices

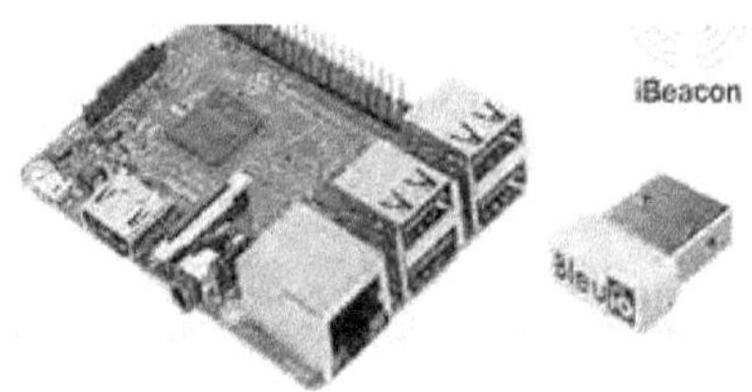

In addition to connecting your Raspberry Pi device to your home internet, you need also to understand how to connect the device to Bluetooth.

There will be moments when you will need to make this happen for many of the projects that we will be focusing on along the road.

This may be as easy as connecting a keyboard or a mouse to the gadget so that you can use it as a typical computer, yet this is not the only limitation.

It will only take a few steps to get things up and running.

The first step is to go to your Pi's screen and look for the Bluetooth icon.

After you've clicked on this icon, check for the option to Add a Device.

Click here, and then go through and search for all of the possibilities offered to you.

Find the one you want to connect with your smartphone, and then follow the instructions that appear on the screen to complete the procedure.

And that is all there is to this entire thing.

Simply by doing a simple search and clicking on the appropriate icons along the way, you can activate Bluetooth on this device and get the Pi to interact with any other Bluetooth-enabled devices that you choose. Once you've gotten these devices to sync with one another, you can get them to function together in the same way that some of the choices on your ordinary computer do.

Remote Raspberry Pi Connection

Finally, we'll look at how we can connect to our Raspberry Pi device remotely.

This is feasible, and there may be times when you're working on a Raspberry Pi and realize you need to access the device remotely. Perhaps you are unable to connect the monitor near you at the moment, or you just need to operate with that device while it is not directly in front of you.

When it comes to the Raspberry Pi gadget, this is something that we can accomplish very simply.

And since we can utilize it just like a conventional computer, the procedure is not too difficult to grasp and operate with.

Some of the alternatives available to you for connecting remotely to the Raspberry Pi are as follows:

- Connect via the command line: You may use SSH from any computer in your house.

  This enables you to use the command line interface on the Raspberry Pi.

  While you won't be able to use a graphical interface with this option, you will be able to execute any command you want via the Terminal.

  The command will be executed on the Raspberry Pi 3 when it is delivered via the Terminal.

  This is a good idea to check out if you have a project that doesn't need a screen to get the job done.

- Use VNC to make another computer the remote screen: If you need to access the Raspberry Pi remotely and use the graphical interface, virtual network computing, or VNC, is your best choice. You will then be able to view the Raspberry device's desktop on your computer's desktop and operate it as required.

This method is a little sluggish, so you shouldn't rely on it all the time.
However, it might be a terrific solution for occasional users to make things simpler.

When you get to this stage, you will know that you have a Raspberry Pi device with all of the necessary setup and settings ready to go.
It should be all set for you to begin working with and using.
We've made sure that the gadget has an operating system that will operate with your Wi-Fi and Bluetooth if you need it, and you can even interact with it remotely to get some of the things done that you want.
With everything in place and ready to go, it's time to move on to the next phase.
We'll now spend some time studying more about the coding and programming that you can do with Pi and this device so that you can truly learn from it and have it set up to perform what you want.

Chapter 3:
Using the Raspberry Pi to Navigate

The next topic will be how to work on traveling through some of the many elements that are located in the Raspberry Pi device.

We spent some time in the previous chapters learning more about this device and what it can accomplish, as well as doing all of the required setup tasks to make it operate.

With everything out of the way, it's time to master the fundamentals of navigating the files, directories, and menus that we'll need to utilize on this device.

Even with a device as easy to use as the Raspberry Pi, there are a lot of files, folders, and menus to deal with, and understanding how to utilize them and even how to work with them will make a great difference in the amount of work that we can get done with this device.

So, let's have a look at them and see what they all imply.

The Crucial Files on the Raspberry Pi
When it comes to this gadget, the first thing we need to investigate and learn more about is the files.

If you want to utilize the command line to modify some of our files, we will need to use the Linux editor.

There are other solutions available for these, including Nano, Vi, and Emacs, so you may compare them.

We'll concentrate on the Nano editor to explore how this works.

It is the default editor that comes with the Raspberry Pi, therefore it is simpler.

You may open this by typing "nano file.txt," and then you can modify the file that you desire.

When you're finished, use CTRL + X to end the application or file.

When you're finished, use CTRL+O to save your work.

To begin, though, we will use the following command to access the necessary files:

/etc/wpa supplicant/wpasupplicant.confsudo nano

This is a crucial file to deal with since it will be the one that modifies our Pi device's Wi-Fi access to the internet.

Then we may go ahead and input the network's name or SSID (if we know it) and password.

Along with these additional characteristics, we can now input a plethora of alternatives to make it simpler to discover the information about the network that we want.

For example, we may provide information such as whether the wireless network is open or concealed, as well as other pertinent details.

Once we've been able to access this specific file, you may proceed to the conclusion of the file, making sure to use the following code to assist:

network = [
ssid="The_SSID_from_earlier"
ask="Your_wifi_password

You may use this to adjust the default settings and get them to fit the characteristics of your network.

To make this work, you must use the "sudo reboot" command to restart the Raspberry Pi.

You may check to see whether you were able to connect to this wireless network on your device by going to the command line and running "ifconfig wlan0."

If the value "inetaddr" is present, it indicates that the device was successfully connected to the wireless network.

If you discover that there is no value there, it is important to double-check the network parameters.

You may do this by use the code provided below.

```
sudo nano /etc/default/keyboard
```

One thing to keep in mind is that the keyboard on the Pi device may be in GB rather than US.

This might create complications with the indications you get.

If you are utilizing any of the codes listed here, please sure to change the keyboard layout from GB to US to guarantee that you receive what you need.

How to Use the Menus in the Desktop Environment

When we work with the excellent Raspbian operating system on this device, you will discover that the concept of menus and other features is rather easy to grasp.

There will be one of the large and primary menus that is easy to access since you just need to click on Raspberry, which is located on the top and left of the screen.

This main menu will include all submenus, such as help, accessories, preferences, games, office, programming, and the internet.

The programming menu is at the top of the list.

This is the section where you'll keep all of the tools you'll need to accomplish development on this device.

This implies that we'll generally find the IDLE Python editor there.

Then we may go to the submenu for the office.

This will include a couple of the additional tools that we'd want to use, such as the LibreOffice tools.

The internet submenu, on the other hand, will provide a handful of the many browsers that are discovered and available on your specific device.

Many individuals like being able to work with some of the gadgets that may be installed on this, but you must exercise care while doing so.

This is because you want to choose games that not only your love and want to play, but also don't take up a lot of space on the Raspberry Pi (remember, memory is limited), and don't need a lot of specific hardware.

There are a number of games available that have been properly converted to function on the Pi device, so this should not be an issue.

Then we'll go to the accessories submenu, which is available.

This is a fantastic location to go if you want to locate a range of tools, such as an on-screen keyboard and other tools that make working on this device simpler.

Then we go to the help submenu, which will give us information and directions if we get stuck.

It will include information, instruction manuals, and guidelines to assist us in using this technology.

The preferences submenu is the next kind of submenu that we may discover here.

This is something you'll get to tinker with a little bit because when you make modifications to the device, you can put stuff here so that it's set up and works the way you want it to.

This is the one that will provide you with all of the information you need about your device's settings.

While we're in this window, bear in mind that there are a couple of various things we can do with it.

For example, you may go in and modify the device's name, select the best method to start up the device (through the desktop or the command line), change your password, activate SSH, and do an auto-login.

These are just a few of the several choices available for you to test and add to the preferences submenu as you continue to work on the device.

As you can see, there are quite a few things that you can do when it comes time to pull out the Raspberry Pi device, and you will be able to easily access all of the files and other pieces that you need.

Playing around with the item is one of the finest things you can do when you first acquire it to ensure that it truly works the way you want it to and to make it simpler to grasp how it works and what you can do with it.

Turn on the device when you have completed the installation of the operating system.

Examine each of the menus and submenus to see what you can find. This will make it easy to see what is on the device and what you can do with it, ensuring that we get the most out of the device before attempting to work on any of the projects that we want to accomplish later on.

Chapter 4:
Using the IDLE to Create Our Python Programs

Now that we've gone through and looked at some of the fun things that we can do with the Pi device, as well as the fundamentals of installing the operating system and more on our Pi device, it's time to get down to business and look at some of the fantastic things that we can accomplish with this device.

And in this chapter, we'll introduce the Python programming language, understand how it works a little bit, how to install it to the Pi device, and then get started with some code that will help us make the device function the way we want it to.

While many programmers will remain with Raspbian as the coding language that they wish to utilize on the Raspberry Pi, many newcomers will discover that working on the Python language is much simpler.

Python is a very simple coding language to learn and is often selected by folks who have never spent any time studying coding in the past.

While there are many reasons why we may love the Python language, such as how simple it is for a novice to learn how to use and write in no time, it will also be powerful enough to get the programs that we need to be done in a short time.

However, before we can go through and develop a program with the aid of this language, we must ensure that we are using the correct IDLE editor on Pi.

In this chapter, we'll spend some time learning how to accomplish just that.

To do this, one of the first steps must be to download the IDLE editor for Python and install it on our device.

The IDLE is something that we can readily obtain from the Python website, which is "https:///python.org/downloads."

The IDLE, which stands for Integrated Development and Learning Environment, is vital for really having a proper environment to type down the programs we desire.

There are several advantages to using the Python language, as well as working with the appropriate IDLE editor to type down the Python scripts that we wish to use.

However, some of the characteristics that we will notice with this specific IDLE, as opposed to some of the others available for Python, are as follows:

1. To write in pure Python, use the Tkinter GUI toolkit.

2. It can run on a variety of systems.

This IDLE is set up to work on Mac OS X, Unix, and Windows, and it will function and appear the same on all of them.

3. It features the Python shell window, which serves as the interactive interpreter, as well as the ability to colorize error, output, and input messages in the code.

4. There is also a multi-window text editor with several features that you will find useful while working on your code.

Auto-completion, call hints, smart indent, Python colorizing, and multiple undo are just a few of the features available.

5. You may search inside any window, search across several files, and change items within the editor window.

6. This IDLE also has a debugger with permanent breakpoints, stepping, and viewing of both the local and global namespaces.

7. It comprises browsers, settings, and other dialogs.

Once you've arrived at the correct website to assist us in downloading the IDLE, you may proceed to choose the version of Python you'd want to work with.

Right now, we'll choose between Python 2 and Python 3.

Other than a few improvements, the changes are minor, yet most users feel that Python 3 is the best choice for them since it is the most current version.

There are a few cases where Python 2 will be the greatest option to work with, so conduct some study to see which is best for your requirements.

After you have completed the download page that we mentioned above and clicked to get this into your machine, it will begin with a nice install here.

Allow a few minutes for the installation to complete.

The IDLE may then be launched by selecting it from the apps menu.

Once we get this IDLE up and running, bear in mind that we will have two major options for writing down all of the Python scripts that we need in this editor.

The first step is to enter the code into our console.

The second is to create a new document, write down the whole program we want, save it, and then execute the code when the time comes.

Both of these strategies are effective, and both pros and novices swear by them.

Often, the decision will be influenced more by the manner that you choose.

When we go to the following part, we'll look at both of these instances and evaluate which one is more likely to work for your requirements, so you can make a choice.

To put it simply, if you aim to discover a solid method to test a portion of your code, or if you are working with a very tiny bit of code, you should write it down in the console to make things simpler.

However, if you want to work with a lengthy piece of code and create a large application, you should use the document instead.

Making Use of Your Console

So, let's look at how we may type down some of the programs that we want to utilize directly in the console.

When we want to create a little piece of code, we'll want to use the console, and we'll have to input it one row at a time.

When we are through completing the row, we may hit the Enter button to go on to the next line.

When you work with this and begin with the def keyword, the computer will detect that we want to build a form of code known as a function.

Once you've typed the function, which we'll show you the code for shortly, you'll need to hit the Enter button to go on to the next line.

When you're through with that function and command, you may invoke it with a string parameter.

Take a look at the code sample below to understand how this will operate.


```
>>>def printString(text):
print (text):
```

```
return
>>>printString("Hello World"):
Hello World
>>>
```

When you go ahead and enter this into your editor, the result of Hello World will appear on your screen.

We'll go into functions in more detail in the next chapter, but this is a nice place to start.

Making a New Document using Code

Writing some basic code that is simply a few lines long, like we did above, will be enough to operate inside the console.

You don't have to go through the same amount of labor as we'll see in a minute simply to create a few lines of code.

However, if we want to develop a whole program on the Raspberry Pi, we must ensure that we can manage some of the revisions and other issues that may arise along the road, and work on it in a document that we can save is a preferable alternative.

When we write down some of our Python programs in a document, we will be able to preserve the many elements that go with it.

In this scenario, we must first launch the IDLE editor, which we previously installed, and then go to the top and left of our screen, where the File is placed.

Then, to proceed, click on New File.

When you click on one of the two alternatives, a new window should appear in which you may work.

The first thing we need to do from here is to save the file that we wish to work with.

You may either save the file by clicking on it or by using the command CTRL+S.

After you've been able to save the file, copy and paste the code from the previous example into the new one.

When the code is complete, you can execute it by selecting the Run option and then selecting either F5 or Run Model.

One thing to keep in mind is that if your file isn't saved, the application will remind us to do so.

When you run the code, it will be executed in the Python Shell or the main window.

As you can see, both techniques for writing down your programs are going to be straightforward and easy to deal with.

The second option, on the other hand, is usually going to be the best one if you want to write out long codes and programs because it will make it easier to save your work as you go, and will ensure that if something goes wrong with the computer or the system while you are working, you will not lose all of that code.

Python Comments: How to Write Them

Before we go any further, we need to have a look at another key aspect of creating Python code, whether on your Raspberry Pi device or another computer system.

And now we'll talk about comments and how they operate in this language.

There may be times while you are working on your programs, whether they are basic or complex when you will need to go through and make a remark regarding a certain area of the code.

This might be a section where you identify the code, explain yourself or another person a little more about what you intended to achieve in that section of the code, or just leave a note of some form in the code. However, even if you are leaving these little comments, you do not want them to interfere with or slow down the program that you are creating at the moment.

To make one of these Python comments function without breaking the remainder of your code because the editor wants to execute it, use the # or hash character and then extend it to the end of the line.

You may use these comments at the beginning of the line or at the end when the remainder of the code for that section is complete.

If you accomplish this correctly, you will be able to write these comments and they will not affect the code or the result that you receive.

In reality, when you type down the code that you want to utilize and execute it, the comments will not be visible or recognized until the program runs.

They are just included as a point of clarification, not as an essential element of the code.

You may include as many or as few of these comments as you like depending on your code.

If you choose, you could put them on every line of code.
The basic guideline here is that you don't want to go through and bring in too many since it makes the code a jumble and makes it difficult to understand.
As we can see, there are several components that come together when we interact with Python code.
We must ensure that the IDLE editor is up and running and functional on our Raspberry Pi in order for it to act in the way in which we need to write programs.
Then we can go through the process and really start writing some Python code to generate the apps that we desire

Python's Fundamental Patterns

Now that we've arrived at this stage, let's have a look at some of the things we can do when we want to create some Python code.

This is an excellent language to work with when we are new to Python and don't know what steps to follow since we have never done any coding before.

That's why we're going to get right in and learn a little bit more about how to accomplish some of the codings that we'll need in this language.

The first thing we'll look at here is some of the fundamental patterns that are necessary while dealing with Python.

One thing you will note about the regular expressions we will discuss in a moment is that you will not be limited to working on a single fixed character to make them function.

They may also ensure that you are actively searching for the necessary patterns.

The following are some of the most typical regular expressions that we might use here:

1. a, X, and 9 —

Ordinary characters just mirror themselves.

The following meta-characters will not match themselves merely because they have a specific meaning: $ *? [] and others.

2. (the period)—This will match any single character save the new line sign "n."

3. w—This is the lowercase w that will correspond to the "word" character.

This might be a letter, a number, or an underscore.

Remember that this is a mnemonic and that it will match a single word character rather than the whole word.

4. b—This is the dividing line between a non-word and a word.

5. s—This will match a single white space character, such as the form, tab, return, newline, or space.

If you type S, you're referring to any character that isn't a white space.

6. = start, $ = end—These will match the end or beginning of your string.

7. t, n, r—These are abbreviations for tab, newline, and return.

8. d—This is the decimal digit for all values ranging from 0 to 9.

Some older regex tools will not support this, so use it with caution.

9. —This will limit how unique the character is.

If you use this if you are unsure if a character has a particular meaning or not, it will be handled the same as any other character.

These are only a few examples of regular expressions that function in Python and may appear in our code.

These are going to be significant patterns that we will be able to work with and learn about in this language, therefore we should experiment with them on the IDLE editor that we currently have installed.

Managing Our Common Expressions

We've previously discussed regular expressions briefly, but it's time to go further and find out what they're all about.

Any Python code you develop will need to include at least a passing reference to these regular expressions.

When it comes to them, the first place we may check is the standard library that comes with Python.

When you want to be able to look at messages and then filter them out, you'll often use regular expressions to aid with your code.

It is also feasible that we will utilize them to construct some programs and then check whether or not a string or a certain portion of the text is located in that code, and whether or not it is able to match up with the regular expression that we are using here.

It will be a straightforward procedure after you have completed the coding in Python, and you can even convert this into some of the other coding languages that you may wish to utilize later.

So, what exactly are regular expressions, and how are you going to learn how to use them inside the code that you wish to write?

When it comes to regular expressions, a smart place to start is to open your text editor and see whether there is a term that has been spelled in two distinct ways in the code.

We'll show you how to utilize regular expressions to accomplish a few things so that misspellings don't become as big of an issue as they migh

A Closer Look at the Loops

Another aspect of this process that we should look at is the loops seen in Python.

These are going to be significant, and they are sometimes compared to the conditional statements that will appear in this language and others, but there are some distinctions.

When you work with these loops, you will be able to clean up your present code significantly, and you will even be able to create a big amount of code in just a few lines, rather than having to type out hundreds of possible lines of code.

To begin with, the loops will be present and extremely useful for any programmer who needs to write code for any program that needs to repeat something a certain number of times or at least repeat itself until the conditions you set in them are met, and you do not want to waste that much time writing the same lines over and over again.

For example, if you're working with code that requires a one-to-ten multiplication table, you don't want to waste time writing down all of those lines again and over.

We can utilize the concept of loops to manage this, and we can accomplish it in only a few lines of code as well.

This may seem to be a lot of work to concentrate on, but it is really rather easy to deal with.

And after you've mastered the technique of doing it all, you'll be able to write many lines of code in only a few lines.

The loop instructs the software to resume reading over the same section of code until a new condition that you specified is fulfilled.

You must include this condition in the code or the computer will freeze because it will continue to loop indefinitely.

There are many sorts of loops that you may use.

And whatever one you select will be determined by what you want to do with the code.

Each of these will work based on what you're attempting to do inside the code.

The three loops that we will examine are the while loop, the for loop, and the nested loop.

The first kind of loop that we will look at in our code here is known as the while loop.

This is the kind of loop we might employ when we want to ensure that our code cycles through the iterations a predefined number of times.

When you layout this kind of loop, you can control how many times these iterations occur to ensure that it functions the way you want it to.

The purpose of this kind of loop is not to have the lines of code become trapped in the cycle an infinite number of times.

Your aim is to ensure that it will run through exactly the amount of times that you specify.

If you're writing code that needs to count from one to ten, you should set up this loop to repeat the iteration 10 times.

With this loop option, the loop will cycle over everything a minimum of once and then check to see whether the requirements have been satisfied or not.

In the example of counting from one to ten, the loop will display the number one, then check to see whether the criteria are satisfied, display the number two, and repeat this pattern until it reaches 10 and determines that the condition is no longer met.

These loops are simpler to write than they seem.

Let's look at some example code to see what we can do to construct one of these while loops in our own code to assist us to understand how to make this work for our needs:

```python
counter = 1
while(counter <= 3):
principal = int(input("Enter the principal amount:"))
numberofyears = int(input("Enter the number of years:"))
rateofinterest = float(input("Enter the rate of interest:"))
simpleinterest = principal * numberofyears * rateofinterest/100
print("Simple interest = %.2f" %simpleinterest)
#increase the counter by 1
counter = counter + 1
print("You have calculated simple interest for 3 time!")
```

Now that we've gotten a chance to look at this kind of loop and understand what it can accomplish for us, it's time to fire up the compiler and try creating the code.

You may then run the code to observe what information appears on the screen.

When you finish writing this one, you should have the output set up so that the user can add in the information that they want, and then the program will do the necessary computations to figure out the interest rates, final amounts, and so on based on the numbers that the user is able to enter into this system.

You, as the programmer, get to go through and decide how many loops you want to execute here, or how many times you want the user to be able to add numbers.

We went through this one such that the loop advanced three times, but you may bring in more or less based on your program's aims. The second choice that we can work with is a for a loop.

The while loop has enough power and strength that we can use it for the majority of our loop requirements in Python; nevertheless, there are a few situations when we need to deal with a loop that is somewhat different from the while loop.

This will take us to the for a loop.

The for loop may be used in a variety of circumstances, and it is considered the most conventional approach of writing and producing the loops that we wish to employ.

When it comes time to utilize the for loop, we must do it in such a way that the user is not the one who comes in and offers the information to this program. Instead, you will select when the loop should come to a halt.

This will make it simpler for the loop to go over the iterations in the precise order that we add them to the loop.

This information will then be shown on your computer screen, and the user will not be required to do anything in the meantime.

A nice example of the code that we can deal with here is:

```
# Measure some strings:
words = ['apple,' 'mango,' 'banana,' 'orange']
for w in words:
print(w, len(w))
```

When working with the for loop example above, you may add it to your compiler and watch what happens when it is performed.

When you do this, the four fruits that appear on your screen will appear in the precise sequence that you have written them down.

If you want them to appear in a different order, you may do that, but you'll need to go back to your code and rebuild them in the correct order, or your preferred order.

You can't modify them after you've written them down in syntax and they're ready to be performed in code.

Then we're ready to proceed to the third type of loop.

This nested loop will take some of the previous loops we discussed to the next level.

However, this opens up many of the various aspects that we want to deal with and allows us to add additional complications along the way.

With the nested loop, we are dealing with the process of taking one loop and ensuring that it is put inside another loop.

Both of these loops will then be allowed to continue continuing indefinitely until they have both had a chance to complete their tasks along the way.

This may seem unusual when we start working on them in some of our programs.

Why would you want to go to the trouble of dealing with two loops and have them run concurrently?

However, there are a plethora of programs that you can make with this, and understanding how to design your nested loops is essential.

For example, suppose you're working with code that requires a multiplication table.

Rather than writing hundreds of lines to do this, as would be required if you did it any other way, you would only need to write a few lines.

And it's a lot simpler to deal with than it seems.

The process of writing this code is straightforward enough. Some of the codes that we may use here are as follows:

#write a multiplication table from 1 to 10

For x in xrange(1, 11):

For y in xrange(1, 11):

*Print '%d = %d' % (x, y, x*x)*

When you get the output of this application, it will look something like this:

*1*1 = 1*
*1*2 = 2*
*1*3 = 3*
*1*4 = 4*

To 1*10 = 2.
Then it would proceed to do the table by twos, as seen below:
2*1 = 2
2*2 = 4

And so on until you reach 10*10 = 100 as your last position in the sequence.
Put this into the compiler and see what happens.
You will just need four lines of code to generate a multiplication table that will appear on your application.
Consider how many lines of code you would have to write to obtain this table the old-fashioned way.
This table was created in a few lines, demonstrating how powerful and useful the nested loop can be.

Taking Care of Your Inheritances

Another item to consider while attempting to develop our Python code is the concept of inheritance.

We have discussed a variety of choices, but we will appreciate the fact that Python is an OOP language and can deal with concepts such as inheritance.

We will be able to work with a process of establishing our parent class, and then using it through the code over and over again, converting it into a child class and making the required adjustments and additions to that second code to help keep our code structured and simple to work with.

When you use inheritance in your code, it simply means that you will take part of your original code, which is known as the parent or base code, and copy it down further into the code, and that new one will be known as the child code or the derived code.

When you first start with the child code that we just worked on, it will be the same as the parent code.

However, we can take this a step further.

The programmer may take the child code that they have and make the alterations and changes that you want.

This allows the child code to perform as desired without having to worry about interfering with the parent class or how it works in the first place.

Working with child code has the advantage of allowing us to make as many modifications and alterations as we like.

This will enable you to make any required updates and tweaks without having to worry about how they will affect the original code from which you borrowed it.

Then there's the advantage of just dealing with one of the inheritance legs, or you can go through and construct a line of these child codes as well.

This may seem to be a complicated code to deal with when you are ready to handle your Python scripts, but it will be a basic code to assist us to discover some of the power that Python provides.

Then you may make whatever modifications you wish along the route. Let's look at some of the code that we can use to develop and interact with our inheritances, which includes:

```python
#Example of inheritance
#base class
class Student(object):
def__init__(self, name, rollno):
self.name = name
self.rollno = rollno
#Graduate class inherits or derived from Student class
class GraduateStudent(Student):
def__init__(self, name, rollno, graduate):
Student__init__(self, name, rollno)
self.graduate = graduate
def DisplayGraduateStudent(self):
print("Student Name:", self.name)
print("Student Rollno:", self.rollno)
print("Study Group:", self.graduate)
#Post Graduate class inherits from Student class
class PostGraduate(Student):
def__init__(self, name, rollno, postgrad):
Student__init__(self, name, rollno)
```

```python
self.postgrad = postgrad
def DisplayPostGraduateStudent(self):
print("Student Name:", self.name)
print("Student Rollno:", self.rollno)
print("Study Group:", self.postgrad)
#instantiate from Graduate and PostGraduate classes
objGradStudent = GraduateStudent("Mainu", 1, "MSMathematics")
objPostGradStudent = PostGraduate("Shainu", 2, "MS-CS")
objPostGradStudent.DisplayPostGraduateStudent()
```

When you type this into your interpreter, you are going to get the results:

```
('Student Name:,' 'Mainu')
('Student Rollno:', 1)
('Student Group:', 'MSC-Mathematics')
('Student Name:', 'Shainu')
('Student Rollno:', 2)
('Student Group:', 'MSC-CS')
```

As you can see, there are a lot of different parts that we can work with when it comes to handling our Python codes, learning how to work with some of this, and ensuring that we can write out some of our codes and use this for some of our programs when it comes to using the Raspberry Pi device.

Chapter 5
How to Make Use of a Raspberry Pi

Now that we've finished working with some of the coding that we can do with the Raspberry Pi device, it's time to take things a step further and learn how to work with this Raspberry Pi along the way.

Setting up the Pi to ensure that it works with the sensors, diodes, and other components that you want might be difficult at times.

However, we will spend some time discussing how we can manage this to ensure that we get the most out of Raspberry Pi.

How to Connect Our Electronics

You will discover that the Raspberry Pi gadget is almost worthless if you have not figured out how to interface with and utilize it at all.

Here, we'll look at the best approach to set up the Pi and ensure that the electronics you wish to utilize are compatible.

This part will teach us more about how to configure the Pi so that it can function properly, whether you want to use it on its own or in conjunction with other devices.

The first option that we must consider is ensuring that we have the necessary equipment to ensure that you can get this to function and then ruin your circuit or even your Raspberry Pi.

The multimeter is one of the instruments we'll need to use here.

It is preferable to deal with a digital one.

You must have one before doing any further work with the circuits using this device.

Keep in mind that the Raspberry Pi gadget will be able to assist us in measuring a variety of things, including voltage, current, and resistance.

This will guarantee that you don't start pumping on the circuit and give the gadget more than it can manage.

However, in addition to the multimeter, we must ensure that we have a few additional components in place to assist us to get started.

Some of them will be:

1. Diodes: This is a semiconductor component that merely permits one current to flow in one direction while preventing it from flowing in the other direction.

2. Light-emitting diodes, or LEDs: This LED functions similarly to a diode, except that it generates light of a certain hue if the current travels in the correct direction.

With LEDs, you may pick from a variety of colors, sizes, and forms.

The length of the leg will decide which leg is positive and which is negative.

3. Capacitors: A capacitor is a component that may be utilized to store part of the electrical energy that you need.

This may be handy when there is a large voltage differential between the two plates and you wish to store energy.

Once the voltage difference has dissipated, the energy that has been stored will be released, ensuring that the Pi device is not harmed.

4. Transistors: A transistor is a semiconductor component used to amplify or switch electricity or electric impulses.

5. Optocouplers: These are useful since they are digital switching devices that allow you to disconnect two electrical circuits from one another.

6. Switches and buttons: These should be self-explanatory.

These are the input devices with which you will engage to ensure that the circuit achieves anything.

Their primary purpose is to open or shut a circuit.

Depending on what you want to do with them, they will come in a variety of shapes and sizes.

Recognizing Communication Protocols

The next thing we want to talk about is some of the available communication protocols.

To ensure that the system we have will function well and that there will be some decent communication between the components, we must ensure that we are following the proper protocols.

There are already a few standards that we may search for, as well as ones that are currently in place and must be followed, to ensure that communication between the Raspberry Pi and external devices is always consistent and coherent.

Our communication protocols will be based on them.

As we walk through this, you'll note that there are a few various sorts of communication protocols that we may use here.

And the distinction between them will make it simpler for us to grasp how we deal with the various notions.

When it comes to these communication protocols, some of the most significant topics that we may deal with include:

1. Bitrate: This is the section that will assist us to specify how many bits are transferred per unit of time.

2. Band rate: While the bit rate may represent the number of bits that we have, the band rate can tell how many symbols are conveyed per unit of time that we wish to employ.

The symbols may individually be any amount of bits that we desire, and this typically relies on the design that we are working with.

3. Parallel communication: When we deal with this one, the bits will be sent out in such a way that only one gets out at the same time.

4. Serial communication: This is a sort of communication in which bits are sent out one at a time.

5. Synchronous serial communication: This is the protocol that we will be able to utilize for serial communication, and all of the data that we will use will be sent out in a continuous and constant stream.

This will need that the internal clocks of the systems that we embed to be synchronized at the same rate for the receiver to receive all of the signals at regular intervals.

6. Asynchronous serial communication: When we deal with this one, we will discover that we do not need a synchronized internal clock.

This data stream will include parts of the start and stop signals that occur before and after transmission, respectively.

When we get the receiver to start with the correct start signal, it will ready them for the incoming data stream.

However, when the signal to stop arrives, it will reset itself so that it can be ready to receive a fresh stream at a later time.

Using Arduino for Real-Time Interfacing

If you are unfamiliar with how to work on this, you will discover that the Arduino microcontroller may be a strong tool to work with.
You'll be able to utilize it, together with the Raspberry Pi, to assist us in working on some of the most exciting projects.
Of course, an Arduino board is required to make all of this work.
To make this all work, you will also need to have a considerable bit of programming skill and proficiency.
Of course, this will take more time than we have included in this handbook, so you must do your own study on the subject if you choose to do so.
Though we won't spend much time in this handbook dealing with this kind of interface, you will see that there are a few crucial considerations to keep in mind, including:

1. If you want to utilize any of the other communication protocols, such as the ones we discussed before, you can perform some interfacing with the Arduino board.
2. The Arduino may also be configured as an IC slave. This implies you'll be able to link back to more than one Arduino board to assist if you choose.
3. You will be able to utilize an easy UART connection. This will be able to support one of these alternatives at a time, allowing you to use a different connection to complete your task.
4. If you want to have a higher-level and faster interaction between the Pi device and the Arduino, you will need to invest some time setting your board as the SPI slave is the ideal route for us to proceed.

This is due to the fact that this connection will only have constraints for the Arduino's clock speed.

How to Record Videos and Images

It is also feasible for us to work with the Raspberry Pi device to get audio, make films, and collect all of the photographs that you want.

Of course, we'll need to add a few more if you want to complete any of these tasks.

You can, for example, use the USB webcam, Raspberry Pi camera, USB audio, or audio HAT.

The first option we have is to utilize the Raspberry Pi to capture photographs and movies.

When we put this up, we have numerous alternatives, such as utilizing the device to aid with home security, robotics, automation, and image or video streaming.

It is also feasible for us to work with high-quality films if you have the proper resources. You will be able to see this stream asynchronously after it has been completed using the device.

The only limitation we'll find here is the time since if you don't have enough storage, you won't be able to film a lengthy movie.

To get started, though, we must first add a camera to your smartphone. You may either use a USB webcam or buy a camera that has been designed particularly to interact with your Pi system.

We will work with the Raspberry Pi Camera option to help make this fast and avoid wasting time with the explanation here, but you will discover that the effort that comes with putting on some of the other camera alternatives will be comparable.

To get started with this procedure, we need to ensure that we can connect the camera of our choosing to the Pi device.

There will be a few various alternatives available to us with this one, including:

1. Turn off the gadget.

Make sure you don't touch the ribbon cable's metal contacts or you'll destroy it.

2. Remove the lens protector.

3. Obtain the CSI connection and carefully lift the housing clip.

This will either be white or black.

4. Insert the CSI cable into the corresponding slot.

5. Now you may press down on the housing clip to secure it in place.

6. With this in place, you may power up the Pi device pack and configure the camera.

You may activate the camera by using the following command:

$ sudoraspi-config pi@erpi

7. Power off the gadget.

If you want to go through and capture photographs, use the following command: pi@erpi $ raspistill -o image.jpg

$ ls -l image.jpg pi@erpi

Of course, this is just the beginning of what we will do when it comes time to set up this system and ensure that it is functioning properly.

It is also feasible for us to go through the process of setting up our home security system or even streaming some films using this function if we so choose.

There are a lot of cool things we can do with the camera and webcam on the Pi device, but there are a few more steps we'll need to go through later to get everything set up and working.

How to Capture and Playback Audio

For the most part, while completing the required work to capture the videos that you want, you must ensure that there is some noise or audio that comes with it for them to operate.

Then there are occasions when you merely want to put in the audio that you wish to utilize.

You may wish to include a speaker, for example, to assist the Pi device in playing music or making other sounds along the route.

And now we'll look at the actions we can take to ensure that we can complete this audio task.

So, in order to get the audio set up and ready to go, we must first have the audio input or output device ready to go.

The great thing to deal with here is that the Pi device will come with its own built-in audio output system in most variants, and it will link directly to the device through the HDMI connector.

However, for input, we will need to operate with an extra device.

Some of the possibilities we have to make this happen are as follows:

1. USB audio: For this project to operate, we must be able to connect an input device with USB audio.

This is possible as long as you choose one that is compatible with certain of Linux's drivers.

You may also use some of the USB webcams we discussed before.

To make it work, we just need to choose one that has a microphone.

2. Bluetooth Audio: The next item that we can utilize here is either an audio input that works directly with Bluetooth or an output mechanism to help link back to the Pi device.

We only need to make sure, like with the last option, that we choose one that is compatible with the Linux system for the greatest outcomes.

HATs for Raspberry Pi 3:

These will be known as the Hardware Attached on Top abbreviation.

You may opt to connect one of these to make use of the many audio capabilities that the Pi device will provide.

If you want to guarantee that the recording you make has audio and works properly, you must first check that the ALSA utility program is installed on your device.

This is a useful software to have since it has the play and record tools that we will need to obtain all of the audio that we need.

If we still need to install this program on our device, we may use the following coding:

```
$ Sudo apt update pi@erpi
$ sudo apt install alsa-utils pi@erpi
```

This should be enough to get it downloaded.

You may need to go through the process of rebooting the Pi device to ensure that it appears on the program the way you want it to.

Now, let's take a brief look at how you may utilize this program and the tools that come with it to record and play the audio that you need for your movies or songs.

To record the audio, just enter the following command:

```
$ record -f ed -D plughw:1,0 -d 10 test.wav pi@erpi
```

Then, when you're ready, use the following command to ensure that the audio is playing:

```
/tmppi@erpi # aplay -D plughw:1,0 test.wav
```

As we can see, there are a plethora of alternatives that we may concentrate on when we bring in the Raspberry Pi device and are ready to make it function for our purposes.

We can perform so many tasks and more with this controller, and as long as we are set up and ready to go, we will most likely have the outcomes that we want in no time.

Chapter 6:
Understanding the GPIO Pins on This Device

While we're looking at the Raspberry Pi gadget and all of the cool things we can do with it, let's take a little detour and look at the pins that come with it.

Several pins come with your board, and the quantity that you will have to deal with is entirely dependent on your specific board and which one you choose to acquire in the first place.

Some boards have more pins than others.

There will be some pins that are the same regardless of the board we choose.

These may be difficult to comprehend if you have never programmed before, but being able to work with the pins and understand what they are used for and why each one is vital will make a huge difference in what we can achieve with these boards overall.

In this chapter, we'll look specifically at the GPIO pins.

These are the ones that are found on all of the Raspberry Pi boards that we want to work with, and they can help us achieve some excellent results with it quickly when we want to utilize it to build some of our projects.

With that in mind, let's look at some of the things we need to know about utilizing GPIO pins on our boards.

When we pull out our Raspberry Pi board and look at it, you must come up with a way to utilize it while also getting it to interface with the outside world.

This capability is made feasible by some of the GPIO pins present on this device.

Because they are critical to the device's operation, there are several improvements that we can see with these pins when we compare prior versions of the Raspberry Pi to some of the current alternatives.

In reality, the most recent version of this gadget, the Raspberry Pi 3, has 40 of these exact GPIO pins.

A reasonable way to think about these pins is that they will be switched on the board, and each of them will have two states to deal with.

These two states are simple to recall since they will either be the input or the output.

If we wish to be able to read data from some of the sensors, such as utilizing a computer to tell us what the temperature is outside, we would be in the state of the input.

However, if we want to utilize this device to connect some LED lights for the project and have them turn on and off, we must use the output pins.

When we speak about some of these GPIO pins on our device, four major colors may help us identify which of the many sorts of pins we are working with at the moment.

The first sort of pin will be red, and it will reflect the amount of power that we can provide to our gadget.

Typically, the voltage ranges between 3.3V and 5V, depending on the device.

The black pins are the next sort of pin that we may deal with.

These will be our grounds and the output, but instead of displaying a light or another activity, they will operate more like a negative terminal of a battery, allowing us to transfer the energy around and cause it to behave the way we want.

The yellow pins are the third sort of pin that we may use.

These are the pins we'll be working with since they'll be the ones we'll be able to program.

Remember that we indicated a few paragraphs ago that we can operate with two states on these pins: output and input.

When we do some of the work with the output, we will have our pins set to HIGH (1) or LOW (0) depending on whether it should have some power with it or not.

When we deal with input, things are a little different.

With this one, based on the status of our output, we will see a 0 or 1, and the sensors will be the ones to turn to when we want to figure this out.

Finally, we'll show you some of the orange pins.

These are useful pins to have since they will allow us to link some of our extra boards to the one we are currently working with.

Whether you want to do this or not will be determined on the kind of project you are doing.

With this in mind, we need to be able to see an example of how all of this can operate.

Let's imagine we're going through anything and want to utilize our Raspberry Pi device to enable us have some control over how an LED light works.

To make this one happen, we'd need to take the following steps:

1. First, we must connect the shorter wire found with our LED light to the appropriate resistor on the board.

2. After that, we'll take the opposite side of our LED light and attach it to the resistor on our Raspberry Pi board's GND pin.

3. The last step is to connect the lengthy wire that has been linked with the LED light to one of the yellow pins (you may pick which one you want to work with here) on the board.

That's all we'd need to do to connect the LED light to our circuit board. There would need to be some code here to complete the setup and ensure that the light will turn on or off.

But the pins that are found on our device will make it easier to hook up any of the extra components that we want, whether they are LED lights or something else, and get the work done.

It will only take a few attempts to complete this project until we grasp how the pins function and what we can do with them.

Chapter 7:
Simple Troubleshooting Techniques for the Raspberry Pi

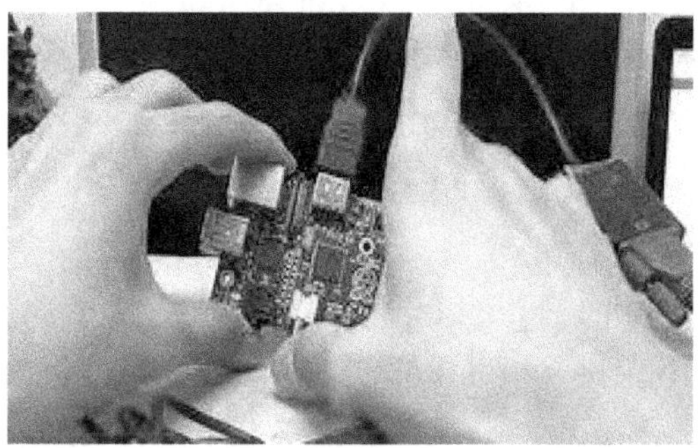

The last thing we need to look at here when it comes to managing our Raspberry Pi device is how to conduct some troubleshooting to get this device to function the way we want it to.

When it comes time to open up that device and get it set up to accomplish the task we want, we have a lot of alternatives to choose from. However, there are instances when the gadget will not operate as we want.

We need to be able to take control of this and make sure we have the right tools to do the proper troubleshooting and get this resolved.

This chapter will assist us in taking a deeper look at a lot of the challenges that may arise when we concentrate on the Raspberry Pi.

The essential thing to remember with this one is that the Raspberry Pi will frequently operate just fine, and if there is a difficulty, it is as easy as changing the pins you are using or ensuring that the code you wrote is correct for what you are doing.

This will let us know that the board will be alright, and there are many choices we can take to get this board to operate if we run into any problems.

When it comes to troubleshooting the Raspberry Pi, the good news is that most of the difficulties are common, and you can repair them yourself rather than hiring an expert or giving up on your board.
Some faults may be as simple as resetting the device, while others may need replacing some of the components you're dealing with, and still, others may necessitate starting over from scratch and determining what went wrong.
However, many times when our Raspberry Pi gadget isn't operating properly, the problem is minor and may be resolved fast.
We'll look at some of the most frequent difficulties with the Raspberry Pi and what we can do to try to address them so that you can utilize your board and get some of the code to function properly for you.

How to Prevent Having a Corrupted SD Card

The first issue that we need to look at, and one of the most typical issues that arise when working with this kind of device, is that we choose an SD card to deal with that ends up being corrupted.

This isn't a typical problem, and as long as you acquire a decent quality card to work with and don't tinker with it too much, it should work well with your Raspberry Pi.

This is frequently an issue that arises when the SD card is a little older since it is unable to manage some of the work that you want to conduct with it.

If this is your first time working with the Raspberry Pi gadget, it may be a good idea to purchase a fresh new SD card.

This is preferable to bringing out one of the older cards, which may be unable to do part of the tasks as readily.

A highly regarded one, such as an SDHC, is an excellent alternative, and be sure it can carry at least 2 GB or more.

The Pi gadget will be able to depend on storage in the same way that most high-end tablets do.

This means you'll need to make sure your SD card is sturdy enough and has enough room to get everything done.

Keep in mind, however, that no matter which of the various SD cards are available to you, other techniques may sneak in and contaminate our data here as well.

The first problem that may arise is attempting to remove the SD card before shutting off the Raspberry Pi device. There are guidelines for properly removing the SD card and other storage alternatives from your Raspberry Pi, just as there are for utilizing USB storage on a Windows computer or with certain other operating systems.

In this scenario, it will be safe to remove your SD card only after the device has completely shut down.

Another difficulty that your SD card might create is when you attempt to power off your Pi device incorrectly.

To guarantee that you are shutting down this device safely and effectively and that you do not wind up with difficulties like a corrupt card or other problems in the process, it is necessary to perform some coding.

To avoid this problem, we may use the command "sudo shutdown -It now."

How to Avoid Relying on a Single Power Source

And now it's time to move on to the second problem that we can address with this one.

The fact that this gadget will depend on the USB mains adapter for power will make us feel comfortable and safe when we use it all of the time, particularly when it comes time to provide some of the power that we need for our projects over to the device.

This is a delusion of security.

We presume that this is safe since the USB ports will be comparable to those found on conventional laptops and PCs, as well as on some of the desktop monitors that we use.

This leads us to assume that we can utilize this connection on our Raspberry Pi device to acquire the electricity that this little computer requires.

This is not a smart idea since we must recognize that the procedure of powering our Raspberry Pi device will not be as straightforward as this. Our device may receive enough power when we work with the USB 2.0 port to boot it up and then run it; however, running tasks that require a lot of processing power, or powering a USB network connection, USB storage, a mouse, and a keyboard (all of which are highly likely to need to be used at the same time when you work on your projects), will frequently end up being too powerful for this source.

If you're using this to help power up the Raspberry Pi device and you discover that it begins to shut itself down straight after you go through the booting procedure, a good thing to check for is that the little computer isn't receiving enough power and you should switch to something else instead.

However, it is normally advisable not to depend on this kind of power source since it will most likely not be sufficient for your requirements.

When this is the case, the first step you can do is to only power the device when you have the appropriate power adaptor to complete the task.

There are many alternatives available for us to utilize here, and we just need to take the time to choose the one that will work best for our tastes when we use the device.

Examining the Cables You Use

The third alternative or problem that we must consider is inspecting the wires with which we are dealing.

Keeping an eye on all of our cablings will be vital all of the time, but it will become even more critical when we intend to utilize some of the custom cases that are compatible with this device.

There are instances when manufacturing issues with the shell and cabling of the whole device might manifest, and when this occurs, we will be forced to operate with incorrect power settings.

It is also likely that the Ethernet and HDMI cables may give us issues as a result of all of this.

Similarly, we must be aware that the adapters with which we want to operate are not always built of high-quality alternatives and materials. And when this occurs, they won't be able to meet part of the power demand that you're expecting in the process.

This is why we must exercise care while dealing with and acquiring cables for use in our projects.

Yes, it is wonderful to save money and obtain some of the less expensive cablings when we conduct our projects, but it may have a bad impact on the projects that we are working on and may result in shorting out or other difficulties.

We may look at an example of how this can be done.

For example, HDMI and VGA cables and adapters may claim to be useful, and the vendor may have made some great claims about the same thing, but flaws might still occur with them.

When they do appear, using such cords will put your device's HDTV or monitor, as well as the device itself, in danger.

This is why you should take care of any additional adapters and components that you decide to buy for your projects.

You should double-check to ensure that the ones you choose will function and can give us the electricity we need to accomplish our jobs effectively, without creating any harm or danger to the Pi device or any of the other components that are connected to it.

When it comes to utilizing our Raspberry Pi gadget, there is one more item we need to spend some time on, and that is the USB cord.

These cables will be built in such a way that they can assist us with a variety of tasks.

However, just because a USB cable is meant to charge your smartphone or another similar device does not indicate that it will be acceptable for powering up the Raspberry Pi.

This is true whether or not you go through the process of connecting the mains adapter to the correct location.

There are a lot of concerns and possible harm that might arise if you are not attentive and choose the incorrect adapters for your projects, as well as when the cables used on this device are not carefully selected.

This may seem to be an easy item to deal with, but we must double-check that we are choosing things that are of better quality and can safeguard our equipment rather than cheaper ones that may end up causing a lot of damage.

If you are dealing with one of these Raspberry Pi devices, you must connect all of the individual elements in the correct order, just like you would with any other conventional or desktop computer.

Before we even attempt to boot up our device for the first time, we must go through and double-check that we have the appropriate cords, peripherals, and storage media to make this work.

Once all of everything is in place, you can start to work on finishing off the remainder of the procedure.

For the most part, the steps we just discussed will be sufficient to ensure that any time your Raspberry Pi device stops working properly, you will be able to get it fixed and back up and running in no time—and if you follow these steps and are careful with how you treat your device, you can save a lot of time and money when dealing with data corruption or reimaging your SD card.

This handbook has spent some time delving into some of the cool things that we can accomplish with the Raspberry Pi gadget.

It is a basic board that assists us in learning more about programming and all of the cool things we can do with it along the road.

With some of the stuff out of the way, it's time to dig right in and look at some of the projects that we can do with this board.

When we work with the Raspberry Pi, we may create a wide range of projects.

In actuality, this is a gadget meant to assist novices in working through some of the more difficult first phases of programming and coding, hence a large number of projects were required.

When it comes to working with the Raspberry Pi device, some of the many projects that we may investigate include:

The Arcade Machine

The first kind of project that we want to look at is how we can take the Raspberry Pi device and make it into our small arcade cabinet where we can play games and other things.

This will give us some practice with what we can do with this device, and you will find that the Raspberry Pi is a good controller to use to make an arcade box because it has the potential to hold a lot of games, especially if you use various SD cards, and it will be simple to design into this type of box.

But, before we do that, the programmer must complete some tasks for this to all happen.

We must also ensure that we have all of the essential equipment and accessories to build our arcade box.

Some of the tools and alternatives we'll need to have on hand while building our arcade box include:

- A gaming controller isn't required, although it can make playing some of the games a little simpler.
- A power source to turn on the device The Raspberry Pi 3 (or whichever Raspberry Pi device you wish to use)
- A good SD card (This card needs to be at least 4GB to make the games work)
- An HDMI cable for connecting your device to a monitor
- A television

The first step is to download the RetroPie games to your PI from the RetroPie website.

We're going to utilize the RetroPie website to assist us to obtain some of the older games we'll need on this device.

Simply download the webpage to your SD card so that it may be installed on the Pi device.

To do so, go to retropie.org.uk/download and choose the version of the Raspberry Pi that you wish to work with.

Allow some time for it to copy to your SD card.

When everything on the SD card is complete, power on the Raspberry device.

While you wait for the gadget to load up, plug in the controller and connect it to the television.

Insert the SD card into the device and wait for it to start up.

If the conversion was successful, you should see the EmulationStation appear on the television screen.

As we begin to work on this stage and see anything appear on the screen, we can go through and ensure that any of the settings that are required here are complete.

Because it may make things simpler, the controller is often the ideal approach to do this.

And while we're working on the controller, we can simply walk through and click on the stuff we need before completing it all.

The first time we do this will take some time since we have never done it before, but the more times we go through it, the quicker the project will go.

After we've gone through and gotten the Wi-Fi linked up and ready to go to our device, and you're certain that you've had it set up and ready to go, it's time to add the ROMS component to this device as well.

It will take a few seconds to get this up and running, but the procedure is straightforward and quite similar to what we did before.

To do this, we must first ensure that we have a good, robust internet connection, or we may utilize an Ethernet cable.

If your connection is weak and the ROMs are stopped, you will be left with a slew of issues to sort out.

It is your decision, however, it is frequently advisable to conduct this section using the Ethernet cable to avoid problems.

Log in to your primary computer.

If you are using a Windows computer, you may open the file manager and enter the simple code "/retropie."

If you are using a Mac computer, go to the finder, pick Go, and then click on Connect to Server.

Then you'd enter the code "smb:/retropie."

Both of them provide the same outcomes; they only have to be carried out somewhat differently on various systems.

At this point, we should have the Wi-Fi and other components correctly linked, and we will be able to handle the ROMS on our device.

We should accomplish this remotely, which means we may utilize the SD card to transfer our selected games, or we can pick which games we will play the most often and have them loaded directly on the Raspberry Pi device.

When you've transferred them using any method, it's ready to start playing.

Making the Device a Phone

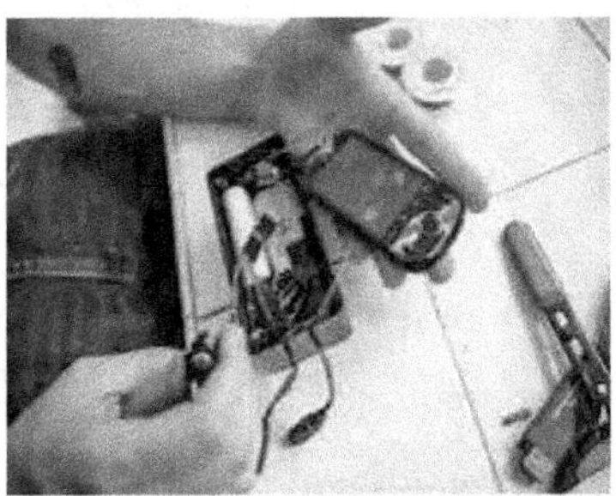

The second project on which we have time is to convert our Raspberry Pi gadget into a phone.

This is much easy than it seems, however, we must bear in mind that it will not be the most modern phone.

We won't be making a smartphone or anything like that, but it will be able to transmit and receive calls as well as to conduct some rudimentary messaging, which might be quite exciting.

To get started with this one, we'll need the following tools:

- Headphones
- Microphone
- An electrical switch
- Velcro squares to help hook it all together
- A touch screen
- GSM module with an antenna and some audio outlets
- Battery pack to help power the phone
- A Raspberry Pi 3 that can handle the Python coding language
- Duct tape
- Cables
- Zip ties
- A sim card
- A converter for DC-DC

- A foam board

When purchasing materials for this project, double-check that they are compatible with the Pi 3 and not another version of the Raspberry Pi. There are several options for materials available, and many of them are less expensive.

However, you must ensure that they are of sufficient quality and that they will function with the gadget that you want to use.

After we have ensured that we have all of the necessary components for our Raspberry Pi device, it is important to ensure that the software we need is also installed on the device.

To make this work, we'll need to bring in the Python we discussed previously, so make sure it's installed on our Raspberry Pi device as well.

While we're at it, we should install a few more pieces of software, such as iPhone and WireHunt, to make it simpler to transform this basic board into the phone we want to use.

The simplest approach for us to add these pieces of software to our device is to first install them to the SD card we wish to utilize and then transfer them over one at a time.

Now that all of these components are there and ready to use, it is time to begin transforming the device into a phone that we can use.

The first step is to connect our battery so that the board, or our phone, can startup.

This must be done via a switch so that the battery receives the appropriate power.

Once it is completed, we may connect both of them to the GSM module.

Take the GSM header and attach it to the converter you're using as well.

Once we've connected all of these, it's time to connect them to the Raspberry Pi device that we'll be working with. We may utilize this in conjunction with some of the other cords that you should have.

The first step is to connect the device to the other transmission pins to guarantee that they remain in contact with one another.

Check that all of the pins are connected to the T and Rx ports.

While this will need us to connect quite a few pieces, once we get this done and can work with the SIM card, we will be ready to go.

Now that all of our lines have been linked and our SIM card has been installed, it is time to go and assemble all of the pieces.

To ensure that this works, we'll need to get out that piece of foam from our list and cut it to the same size as our Pi device.

Place the gadget on top of the foam, and then secure the two sections together using Velcro squares and duct tape.

This step is critical because it will allow us to connect the converter, switch, and module to the opposite side of our piece of foam. When you add the battery pack, make sure it goes someplace secure, generally somewhere between the Pi device and the screen.

You don't want it to move about and create problems.

If it moves, the phone will switch off at random, causing problems along the road.

At this point, assuming you went ahead and connected all of the pieces correctly, you should see that our phone is done for the most part, and you should be able to turn it on and get it to operate.

Turning on the phone is as simple as turning on the switch that leads to it.

From here, you may wait for it to switch on and start-up before dialing any number and making a basic phone call to someone else.

As we can see, this is going to be a straightforward phone to use.

We simply set it up to perform some basic tasks, and it won't be all that sophisticated or have any of the capabilities that we desire or are accustomed to with some of the other phones we've used in the past. But, just like a conventional phone, we can utilize this simple phone to help us create and then receive the codes that we need.

The cool part is that we can take this a step farther if we want.

We're keeping things basic for this project by using a phone that can make and receive calls.

However, it is possible to configure this basic phone to do other functions like texting, browsing the internet, and much more.

This only goes to show that the Raspberry Pi is capable of handling a wide range of tasks, and it can even go far enough to assist us in making our phones with a few easy steps.

While we only had time in this chapter to go over and work on two projects, you can see that there is a lot of diversity that we can enjoy when it comes to utilizing the Raspberry Pi device.

It is easy to operate, and we can do a great deal with only a few affordable accessories.

We can utilize it to develop an arcade game to play some of our old favorite games everywhere we go, and it can even let us make calls with our phones.

And there are a plethora of additional projects that we can carry out with the same concept and a few different attachments along the road.

Conclusion

Thank you for reading through Raspberry Pi; we hope it was educational and provided you with all of the tools you needed to reach your objectives, whatever they may be.

The next step is to begin experimenting with the Raspberry Pi gadget for your purposes.

There are a lot of cool things we can do with the Raspberry Pi, and you are only limited by your programming expertise (which the Raspberry Pi gadget will assist increase) and your creativity.

This is the ideal tool for anybody who wants to learn how to program and do cool things with technology but is hesitant to take the plunge due to a lack of understanding.

This guidebook spent some time looking more carefully at all of the numerous things we can accomplish when it comes to utilizing the Raspberry Pi device for some of our purposes.

We looked at what this gadget is all about and some of the advantages we may get from using it for programming.

We also looked at how to link it to some of the other components that you'll need, such as USB drives, Wi-Fi, and so on, so that we can make some of the projects that we desire.

In addition, we looked at some of the important programming aspects that we should keep in mind as we go through this process.

We concentrated on the Python programming language and some of the things we can accomplish with it.

It is a basic coding language that we can learn as beginners, and you will discover that it is one of the greatest possibilities to assist you out when it comes time to work on the Raspberry Pi, along with many other coding options along the road.

When it comes to utilizing the Raspberry Pi device, there are a lot of various things that we can accomplish, and you will discover that this is the ideal device to help us get started with programming, particularly if we are complete novices.

When you're ready to start programming with the Raspberry Pi and learning how to perform some of your Python programs, be sure to check out this handbook.

Finally, if you found this book beneficial in any way, please leave a review on Amazon.

9 783986 539498